THE CHECKLIST CHALLENGE GUIDE TO ✓ FRIENDSHIP

BY STEPHANIE PETERS

Raintree is an imprint of Capstone Global Library Limited, a company incorporated in England and Wales having its registered office at 264 Banbury Road, Oxford, OX2 7DY – Registered company number: 6695582

www.raintree.co.uk
myorders@raintree.co.uk

Text © Capstone Global Library Limited 2024
Paperback edition published in 2025

The moral rights of the proprietor have been asserted. All rights reserved. No part of this publication may be reproduced in any form or by any means (including photocopying or storing it in any medium by electronic means and whether or not transiently or incidentally to some other use of this publication) without the written permission of the copyright owner, except in accordance with the provisions of the Copyright, Designs and Patents Act 1988 or under the terms of a licence issued by the Copyright Licensing Agency, 5th Floor, Shackleton House, 4 Battle Bridge Lane, London, SE1 2HX (www.cla.co.uk). Applications for the copyright owner's written permission should be addressed to the publisher.

Editorial Credits
Editor: Donald Lemke; Designer: Kay Fraser; Media Researchers: Jo Miller and Svetlana Zhurkin; Production Specialist: Katy LaVigne

ISBN 978 1 3982 5213 4 (hardback)
ISBN 978 1 3982 5214 1 (paperback)

British Library Cataloguing in Publication Data
A full catalogue record for this book is available from the British Library.

Image credits
Getty Images: Alex Potemkin, 25, Cavan Images, 24, fstop123, 4, kali9, 21, Robert Niedring, 11, xavierarnau, cover (bottom left); Shutterstock: Antonio Guillem, 15, Asier Romero, 23, BearFotos, 14, Daisy Daisy, 20, Diego Cervo, 27, Elena Elisseeva, 26, Ground Picture, 10, 12, Inside Creative House, 7, LightField Studios, 13, Max Kegfire, cover (right), Monkey Business Images, cover (bottom right), 16, 18, MPH Photos, 5, New Africa, 9, P Maxwell Photography, 29, Prostock-studio, 8, Rido, 17, Tanya Terekhina, 28, VH-studio, 6, ViDI Studio, 22, zentilia, 19

Every effort has been made to contact copyright holders of material reproduced in this book. Any omissions will be rectified in subsequent printings if notice is given to the publisher.

All the internet addresses (URLs) given in this book were valid at the time of going to press. However, due to the dynamic nature of the internet, some addresses may have changed, or sites may have changed or ceased to exist since publication. While the author and publisher regret any inconvenience this may cause readers, no responsibility for any such changes can be accepted by either the author or the publisher.

Printed and bound in India.

CONTENTS

BUDDY SYSTEM 4

MEET AND GREET 101 6

BFFS OR A BUNCH OF BUDS? 12

THE COLOURS OF FRIENDSHIP 18

IF THINGS GO WRONG 24

WANT TO TRY MORE? 28

GLOSSARY 30

FIND OUT MORE 31

INDEX 32

ABOUT THE AUTHOR 32

Words in **bold** appear in the glossary.

☑ BUDDY SYSTEM

What does it mean to be a good friend? How do you make new friends? Check out some useful tips and fun facts in this guide. Take the checklist challenge and create long-lasting friendships!

☑ MEET AND GREET 101

Meeting people for the first time can be scary. Tackle that fear by focusing on friendly **gestures**. Learning how to put your best foot forward is a great checklist item!

SMILE

Making friends starts with a smile. Add a handshake or fist bump — and *BOOM!* You're both closer to making a new friend.

DID YOU KNOW?

Ancient Greeks shook hands to show they came in peace. Their empty hands proved that they didn't carry weapons.

WHAT'S IN A NAME?

Take time to learn someone's name. It tells that person that they matter to you. So add "remembering names" to your friendship checklist! If you forget a name, just ask. That person has probably forgotten a name before too.

SAME (AND NOT SAME)!

Good friends often like the same things. But it's okay if you don't! Opening yourself up to new experiences is a great checklist item. Take time to find out the stuff your friend likes. You could end up liking those things too.

☑ BFFS OR A BUNCH OF BUDS?

Friendships work best when you know yourself first. Make it a checklist item to understand what's important to you. Once you know that, opening up to others will be easier.

FRIEND COMFORT ZONE

Extroverts love being part of a large friend group. **Introverts** are happy having one or two best friends. Understanding your friend comfort zone can go on your checklist.

QUALITY Q&A

Get to know someone better by asking questions about them. Listen carefully to the answers. Ask follow-up questions if you want to know more. Being a good listener is a key to strong friendships. Add it to your checklist!

JOIN THE CLUB

Want to grow your friend group? Clubs are a great place to meet people who share your interests. Start by joining clubs at your school or in your town. Or add "Start My Own Club" to your checklist! Then create a club for your favourite hobby or sport.

✓ THE COLOURS OF FRIENDSHIP

What makes a good friend? When should you think about walking away from a friendship? Understanding the difference between a good and a bad friendship can help. It's an excellent idea for your checklist.

GREEN LIGHTS

Green means *go*! Green-light friends are honest and **supportive**. When you meet someone with these traits, you should *go* with that friendship!

Show your friend you trust them to steer you in the right direction!

RED FLAGS

Red flags are warning signs that something is not right. **Gossiping**, starting **rumours**, telling secrets and making fun of others are all red flags. If someone shows these flags, you might need to decide if that person is really your friend.

GREY AREAS

Sometimes friends encourage you to try new activities. But what if a friend **pressures** you into doing something you think is wrong? A true friend will understand if you say no. Still, saying no can be hard. Learning how can be an item on your checklist.

 IF THINGS GO WRONG

What do you do when a friendship is in trouble . . . or over? It might be difficult to let go. But it's important to accept when a friendship has run its course. Learning how to say goodbye to a friend should be on every friendship checklist.

ARE WE CALLING IT QUITS?

Friendships end for many reasons. Maybe you moved away and lost touch. Maybe you're not interested in the same things any more. Whatever the reason, it's hard to lose or let go of a friend.

FRIENDS MAKE UP

Arguments between friends — even best friends — can happen. The first step to patching things up is talking about it. A good checklist goal is learning to admit your mistakes, make and accept apologies and then move forward.

WANT TO TRY MORE?

You've got all the important checklist items for making some solid friendships! Now it's time to add some fun activities and experiences to your must-do list. Check out (and then check off) a few of these ideas. Then think of other items to add to the list. A checklist is always changing and growing – just like you and your friendships!

- ☑ Share friendship bracelets.

- ☑ Make up a silly story together.

- ☑ Create a social media video.
- ☑ Go to a friend's special event.
- ☑ Make a silly sign to cheer on a friend.
- ☑ Go camping – inside or outdoors!
- ☑ Invite others into your friendship group.
- ☑ Make a huge ice cream sundae and ENJOY!

GLOSSARY

extrovert sociable person who enjoys being with many other people

gesture movement usually of the body or limbs to express or emphasize an idea or attitude

gossip conversations or reports about other people involving details that are not confirmed as being true

introvert shy person who prefers to spend time alone or with a few people

pressure strong influence or force

rumour talk or opinion widely spread with no real source

supportive providing encouragement or emotional help

FIND OUT MORE

BOOKS

Be Confident Be You, Becky Goddard-Hill (Collins, 2023)

Life Skills for Tweens (Essential Life Skills for Teens), Ferne Bowe (Bemberton, 2023)

You Are a Champion: How to Be the Best You Can Be, Marcus Rashford (MacMillan, 2021)

WEBSITES

kidshealth.org/en/kids/peer-pressure.html#catfriend
This website has advice on how to deal with peer pressure.

www.bbc.co.uk/bitesize/articles/z6mj47h
Check out the friendship guide on the BBC Bitesize website.

www.childrenssociety.org.uk/sites/default/files/2020-10/friendship-guide-for-young-people_0.pdf
The Children's Society has made a friendship guide with lots of useful advice.

INDEX

activities 10, 28–29
arguments 26

clubs 16

ending friendships 24–25
extroverts 13

gossip 20
greetings 6–7

handshakes 7
hobbies 16

introverts 13

listening 14

names 9

peer pressure 22

red flags 20
rumours 20

ABOUT THE AUTHOR

Stephanie Peters has been writing books for young readers for more than 25 years. Among her most recent titles are *Sleeping Beauty: Magic Master* and *Johnny Slimeseed*, both for Raintree's Far-Out Fairy Tales and Folk Tales series. An avid reader, workout enthusiast and beach wanderer, Stephanie enjoys spending time with her children, Jackson and Chloe, her husband, Dan, and the family's two cats and two rabbits. She lives and works in Mansfield, Massachusetts, USA.